CW00997028

Bacon Recipes:

The Ultimate Bacon Cookbook

Ellen Scott

© 2014 Ellen Scott. All rights reserved.

No part of this publication may be reproduced in any way whatsoever. The author of this book does not dispense medical advice or prescribe the use of any technique as a form of treatment for physical, emotional, or medical problems without the advice of a physician, either directly or indirectly.

The information in this book reflects the author's opinions and is in no way intended to replace medical advice.

The author has made every effort to provide accurate information in the creation of this book. The author accepts no responsibility and offers no warranty for any damages or loss of any kind that might be incurred by the reader/user due to actions resulting from the use of the information in this book.

The user assumes complete responsibility for the use of the information in this text.

Table Of Contents

Introduction

What comes to your mind when you hear the word "bacon"? Isn't it breakfast? Most of us will get hungry imagining a hearty breakfast of eggs, bread, hash browns and, BACON. Who would want to miss such a delightful morning meal?

Since it is versatile enough to be used in every other recipe and delicious enough to stand on its own, bacon is an essential part of meals for most foodies, including me.

Still wondering why?

Because this simple food is a great combination of texture and flavor. Crisp, salty, smoky and just indulging, having bacon for breakfast is just the best. From maple or peppered to hickory and honey - you have a whole variety to choose from.

While most people will think that bacon is oily – and therefore high in fat and cholesterol, I would say that your body really needs bacon, as bacon is taken from pork, which is a high-protein meat.

At the end of the day, I love my bacon and I want to share some simple and delicious ways to prepare it!

In this book, I've shared my favorite bacon recipes for breakfast, lunch, dinner. There are several sections- including recipes for each meal of the day plus a bonus section of very quick, snack recipes.

Feel free to use these recipes for other times- there are no rules that say you cannot have bacon pancakes for dinner or bacon-cheddar biscuits for breakfast.

Some of these recipes might technically freeze well for long term storage but they are so delicious that you will hardly want to wait to have your meal!

Breakfast Recipes

Bacon and Egg Breakfast Treat

Ingredients:

4 English muffins (can use whole wheat muffins if you would like)

8 slices of smoked back bacon

4 large eggs

4 slices of cheese (any kind that you like)

Directions:

Brown the bacon on all sides in a non-stick skillet

sprayed with cooking oil.

Remove from the pan and set on a layer of paper towel to drain.

Wipe out the skillet and lightly respray.

Spray four cooking rings (See note below) and then add one egg to each ring.

Cook until each is done to your personal taste, keeping in mind that a runny egg will make your sandwich slightly soggy.

While the eggs are cooking, you can toast each of the four English muffins and then top them with the slices of cheese.

For extra cheesy flavor, you can double the amount and add a slice to each side of the muffin.

Layer the hot eggs and the bacon on the toasted muffin and enjoy.

Optional: you can add other ingredients to these breakfast sandwiches. Try something like sliced tomato or onions.

Note: If you do not have the cooking rings ,you can make your own with cuffs of rolled aluminum foil. Be sure to spray these extra well because the eggs are more likely to stick.

You can also make the eggs in a mug in the microwave to get the round shape- just crack an egg into a sprayed mug and then poke the yolk with a fork.

Egg & Bacon Pie

Ingredients:

5 strips of bacon, crisped and crumbled

1 small diced onion

1/3 cup of creamy goat cheese

1 frozen pie crust (9 inch)

4 whole eggs plus 4 more egg whites

½ cup of milk

1 tablespoon of butter

1 tablespoon of Dijon mustard

6 halved cherry tomatoes

Directions:

Preheat oven to 325.

Sauté the onions in the butter until they are soft and translucent.

Remove from heat and add the goat cheese, mixing well.

Layer this into the prepared crust.

Whisk the eggs and the milk and then add in the Dijon mustard, mixing well.

Pour the milk and egg mixture over the goat cheese mixture in the pie crust.

Bake for 20 minutes or until it is just starting to get firm at the edges. The middle will still have a bit of jiggle to it.

Sprinkle the crumbled bacon over the top of the pie

and then arrange the tomatoes as you see fit.

Bake the pie for another 15 minutes.

Once it is removed from the oven the pie should be allowed to rest for five minutes before cutting and serving.

Optional: sprinkle the pie with chives just as it comes out of the oven.

Note: you might consider baking this pie on a baking sheet as it makes removing it from the oven for the second step easier and prevents the risk of spillovers.

Baconuits: Bacon Cheese Biscuits

Ingredients:

6 slices of thick cut bacon, diced into cubes

1 cup of all purpose flour

1 cup of cake flour

2 teaspoons baking powder

½ teaspoon baking soda

1 ½ teaspoon sugar

8 tablespoons or one stick of chilled butter

1 cup of shredded sharp or mild cheddar cheese

¼ cup diced onions or chives

1 cup of heavy cream or buttermilk

Directions:

Preheat oven to 450.

Fry the bacon until it is crisp in a cast iron skillet. Drain the bacon on a layer of paper towel.

Reserve 1 tablespoon of the pan drippings and then discard (or save) the rest.

Add the dry ingredients to a food processor or a large bowl. Pulse or whisk to combine.

Cut the butter into cubes and then add to the dry ingredients. If using a food processor, pulse a few times. If not, you can use a pastry cutter or two forks to cut in the butter.

Add all but the cream and combine.

Add in the cream and mix until everything is well

blended and there is no more dry flour remaining. Form the dough into a ball.

Turn the dough out onto a lightly floured surface and roll out into a circle that is about three-fourths of an inch in thickness.

Using a round biscuit cutter make as many biscuits as the dough allows, rerolling the scraps as needed.

Arrange the biscuits into the same cast iron skillet that you used to fry the bacon and brush the tops of each with the reserved bacon drippings.

Bake for 20 minutes.

Delicious Bacon Pancakes

Ingredients:

1 cup of all purpose flour

2 Tablespoons sugar

1 ½ teaspoon baking powder

½ teaspoon baking soda

1 ¼ cup buttermilk

2 tablespoons melted butter

1 large egg

8 slices of bacon, fried and reserved. Reserve 1 teaspoon of the drippings and drain the rest.

Directions:

Set the oven to 200 degrees.

Whisk the dry ingredients together in a large bowl. Whisk the milk, butter and eggs in a separate bowl and then whisk the flour mixture into the wet mixture.

Only mix until combined- there should be some lumps remaining in this batter.

Heat a non-stick skillet to medium and then add ¼ cup of the batter.

Top the uncooked batter with one slice of the bacon and cook the pancake until bubbles start to form and the edges start to dry out.

Flip carefully and continue cooking until the pancake is cooked all the way through.

Transfer to a platter and cover loosely with foil. Put

the platter in the warm oven while continuing to cook the rest of the pancake batter.

Lunch Recipes

Family Fav Meatloaf

Ingredients:

1 to 1 ½ pound ground beef

1 pound ground veal

1 chopped onion

2 tablespoons of fat of your choice(olive oil, butter, coconut oil, bacon grease)

1/3 cups sour cream

1 tablespoon Worcestershire sauce

½ cup bread crumbs

2 tablespoons chopped, flat leaf parsley

Pinch each of thyme and marjoram

Pepper & salt to taste

2 whole eggs

3 or 4 slices of bacon

¼ cup of barbeque sauce, your choice of style, flavor and brand.

Directions:

Preheat oven to 375

Line a baking pan with foil and then spray the foil with cooking spray

Mix the two ground meats together. Add the onion and your choice of fat to the meats.

Whisk the eggs and the Worcestershire sauce together before adding to the meat mixture.

Using your hands, combine everything well and then form into a loaf of the desired thickness. (This may depend in part on the size of your pan.)

Bake for thirty minutes and then remove from the oven. Drain off any of the accumulated fat before placing bacon strips across the meatloaf. Bake for 15 more minutes.

Once again remove from oven and if necessary, drain again. Slather on the barbeque sauce and bake for 15 to 20 more minutes. Let the meatloaf rest for 5 to 10 minutes when brought out of the oven for a final time and then serve.

Note: you can also add cheese to this recipe if you would like. You can add your favorite type of cheese in the middle of the meatloaf or layer it on top before the bacon, your choice.

Pizza with Bacon & Eggs

Ingredients:

Six ounces of thick cut bacon, cut into 1/3 inch portions

4 large eggs

1 tablespoon heavy cream

2 tablespoons butter

Flour for dusting

I pound of pizza dough (you can also use a premade dough to save time)

1/3 cup crème fraiche

3 ounces of Brie

2 ounces of shredded fresh mozzarella

Chives for garnish

Directions:

Preheat oven and pizza stone to 500

Place bacon in a pie plate and bake until it is crispy, about fifteen minutes. Drain and reserve.

Whisk the eggs and heavy cream together in a small bowl and set aside.

Cook the eggs in half of the butter until small curds have formed and the eggs take on a creamy appearance.

Remove the pan from the heat. Stir in the remaining half of the butter and season with salt to taste.

If you are using dough then stretch it on a floured

surface to a 12 inch round and transfer to a pizza peel.

Spread with the crème fraiche making sure to leave a one inch border all the way around. Top with the bacon and two cheeses.

Slide the pizza onto the preheated pizza stone and bake for about 7 minutes.

Remove from the oven and add the eggs. Put back into the oven for another 2 minutes and then remove. Immediately garnish with the chives and serve hot.

Note: if you do not have a pizza peel and/or a pizza stone you can use a round pizza pan. You can also do this pizza on a grill following the basic steps above.

More Than Your Basic Bacon Burgers

Ingredients:

½ cup of beer (any type, any brand)

1 pound ground beef (lean meat)

¼ cup bread crumbs

¼ to ½ of an onion (your choice of yellow or white. The amount depends on the size of the onion and how much onion flavor you like in your burgers)

1 tablespoon Worcestershire sauce

1 teaspoon Dijon or spicy brown mustard

¼ teaspoon liquid smoke

½ teaspoon powdered garlic

Salt & pepper (according to your preference)

4 to 6 hamburger buns, any style

4 to 6 slices of any style of bacon, fried and drained

Toppings of your preference

Cheese of your choice

Directions:

Combine all ingredients except for the bacon, toppings and buns (of course) in a bowl being sure to mix everything very well.

Shape your burgers into round patties that are about an inch thick or so. (You might like a slightly thicker or thinner burger). Grill or pan fry until the burgers are cooked all the way through and then top with cheese.

Either close the grill lid or place a lid over the pan to melt the cheese and then top with bacon and your choice of toppers.

Note: these burgers can be made ahead and frozen if you would like. After making the patties, wrap each in plastic wrap and then place in a freezer bag.

Brown Sugar Pork Loin Wrapped in Bacon

Ingredients for the Pork Loin:

3 pounds of pork loin roast

5 to 6 strips of bacon

Ingredients for the Spice Rub:

½ teaspoon chili powder

¼ teaspoon hot Spanish paprika

¼ teaspoon ground cumin

½ teaspoon cinnamon

Ingredients for the Brown Sugar Glaze:

½ cup dark brown sugar

1 tablespoon flour

1 tablespoon apple cider vinegar

¼ teaspoon mustard powder

Directions:

Preheat oven to 375. Line a pan with foil.

Combine all of the ingredients for the spice rub together and then rub over the entire surface of the pork roast. Roast for 50 to 60 minutes.

While the tenderloin is baking make the glaze by stirring all of the ingredients in a small pan.

Simmer until all of the sugar dissolves.

Drizzle over the pork loin after the first 50 to 60 minutes of baking time is up and then continue baking another 25 to 25 minutes or until a thermometer reaches 160 degrees.

Let your pork loin rest for ten minutes before serving.

Fun Bacon Pizza For All

Ingredients for the Sauce:

¼ cup balsamic vinegar

½ cup strawberry jam or preserves

1 teaspoon siracha chili sauce

Ingredients for the pizza toppings:

Small amount of olive oil for brushing

1 cup of shredded or diced, cooked chicken

4 slices of cooked, apple wood smoked bacon, diced

1/2 cup thinly sliced onion

4 ounces shredded mozzarella

2 ounces freshly grated parmesan cheese

2 to 3 tablespoons of fresh cilantro, finely minced

½ cup hulled, fresh strawberries, diced.

Pizza dough- your choice of homemade or storebought

Directions:

Make the sauce by heating the balsamic vinegar in a small saucepan over medium to high heat, bringing to a full boil.

Once it boils, reduce the heat and continue to simmer for four to five minutes until it is reduced in volume by about half.

The sauce should be thick and syrupy at this point.

Remove from heat and add in the jam and the chili sauce.

Preheat the oven to 500 degrees. If using a pizza stone preheat for thirty minutes.

If using a homemade dough roll out to a 12 to 14 inch round and lightly brush with olive oil. If using a premade dough then skip ahead to the olive oil step.

Spread the sauce onto the dough and then add the chicken, bacon, onions, cheese, cilantro and strawberries.

Bake until the crust is starting to turn golden brown and the cheese is melted and bubbly.

Cauliflower & Bacon Soup

Ingredients:

½ head of cauliflower

3 cups of broth (homemade if you have it. Canned, good quality broth of any type is also fine.)

2 slices of bacon

2 tablespoons of crumbled gorgonzola cheese

Directions:

Steam the cauliflower until it is very tender. (You can do this in the microwave)

Cook the bacon until it is crisp and then mince it.

Heat the broth in a microwave safe bowl.

Drain the cauliflower and put it into a blender or food processor with the warmed broth.

Process on high until it is very smooth.

You may need to add more broth if it seems too thick.

Garnish with the minced bacon and the crumbled gorgonzola cheese.

Bacon Style Garlic Pinwheels

Ingredients:

2 to 2 ¼ cup all-purpose flour

1 package of rapid rise yeast

2 tbsps sugar

2 tbsps of butter

¼ cup of water

½ cup of milk

Toppings:

2 cups of triple cheese blend with cream cheese
(This is a packaged, shredded cheese which has
cream cheese already added)

1 pound of bacon fried until crisp and then chopped into rough pieces

2 tsps of chopped garlic

4 tbsps melted butter

½ tsp parsley

Directions:

Place ¾ cup of the flour, the undissolved yeast, salt and sugar in a bowl.

In a small saucepan, over low to medium heat, heat the milk, butter and water to very warm and then add to the flour mixture.

Now you need to beat this with an electric mixer on medium speed for about two minutes being sure to scrape the sides of the bowl frequently.

Add another ¼ cup of the flour and then beat on high for another two minutes.

Then, stir in the remaining flour just enough to make perfectly soft dough.

Knead the dough on a floured surface until the dough becomes elastic and smooth.

This should take about eight to ten minutes. Now roll the soft dough to make a 9 x 13'' rectangle and spread with 2 teaspoons of melted butter.

Evenly spread the shredded cheese (one cup) on top of the dough and then top that with ½ of the bacon.

Roll the dough starting from one of the short sides.

Cut into 12 even pieces by cutting the rolled dough in half. Cut each half in half again. Cut each of those sections into three pieces.

Grease your baking pan and set aside.

Drizzle the pinwheels with butter and garlic and then cover loosely.

Allow the dough to rise thirty minutes or when you see it has doubled in size. Bake at 375 for twenty minutes.

Sprinkle on the remaining bacon and cheese and bake for another five minutes.

Dinner Recipes

Bacony Pasta

Ingredients:

4 to 5 slices of bacon

½ onion (yellow or white) thinly sliced

½ pound of pasta, any variety, any shape

3 medium yellow squashes, peeled, seeded and cubed

3 ounces of goat cheese

Small handful of fresh basil cut into ribbons.

Seasoning to taste

Directions:

Cook the bacon in a huge skillet until it is crispy. Remove from pan and set aside to drain.

Add the onions to the bacon grease in the pan and season accordingly.

Cook until the onions are softened and lightly browned. Add in the squash and continue cooking.

Meanwhile, bring salted water to boil for the pasta.

Cook the pasta according to the directions on the pasta. Save ½ cup of the pasta cooking water for later.

Drain the pasta before adding to the squash and onions. Crumble the goat cheese on the top of this and stir to combine.

Add in the reserved pasta water to make a nice, creamy sauce. Crumble the cooked bacon over the top, add in the fresh basil ribbons and adjust the seasoning to your taste.

Red Lentils and Bacon Soup

Ingredients:

1 tablespoon olive oil

2 packages pancetta cubes. (If you cannot find pancetta cubes you can use smoked ham or thick cut bacon)

1 onion, diced

1 carrot, diced

1 teaspoon cumin

½ teaspoon turmeric

2 cloves of fresh garlic, chopped

1 sliced chili

2 stock cubes (any flavor)

2 cans of red lentils, rinsed.

Directions:

Heat the olive oil in a large pan and then add the onions and one package of the pancetta (or half of the ham or bacon if that is what you are using).

Add in the carrot and cook on low/medium until the onions are starting to soften.

Add the spices and cook for another minute or two. The pan should be very fragrant at this point.

Pour in about 4 to 4 ½ cups of water and crumble in the stock cubes that you are using.

Add the lentils and simmer for twenty minutes stirring occasionally.

Fry the remaining pancetta for ten minutes or until

it is nicely crisped up. Serve the soup with this crispy pancetta on top.

Bacon Quiche

Ingredients:

3 large eggs, beaten

1 ½ cup heavy cream

Seasoning to taste

2 cups of fresh baby spinach, chopped and packed

1 pound of bacon, any style, cooked and crumbled.

1 ½ cup shredded Swiss cheese

1 9 inch pie crust (homemade, refrigerated or frozen)

Directions:

Preheat oven to 375

Combine the eggs, heavy cream and seasoning in a small bowl and set aside.

Layer the spinach, bacon and cheese in the pie crust and then pour the egg mixture over top. Bake for 35 to 45 minutes.

Bacon Wrapped Haddock

Ingredients:

1 large haddock fillet

9 slices of bacon

1 lemon

Freshly cracked black peppercorns

Directions:

Preheat oven to 425

Prep a pan by placing a baking rack on top of a baking sheet and set aside.

Cut the haddock into three equally sized pieces and season with the fresh black pepper. Wrap each of these three pieces of fish with three pieces of bacon and then place seam side down on the prepared pan.

Cook for 12 minutes and the carefully flip over and cook the other side until the bacon is browned. Once the bacon is done, the fish is done.

Remove from the oven and squeeze lemon juice on each. Serve with your side dishes and more lemon wedges.

Corn Cakes with Bacon

Ingredients:

2 tablespoons plus 1 teaspoon of olive oil

2 cups of fresh corn (You can use thawed, frozen corn in this recipe but not canned corn)

1 diced zucchini

8 slices of bacon (any style)

2 thinly sliced scallions

2 large eggs, lightly beaten

¼ cup cornmeal

2 ounces crumbled goat cheese

Seasoning to taste

Directions:

Heat 1 teaspoon of olive oil in a skillet. Make sure that you're using medium heat to cook.

Add the fresh corn and the zucchini along with salt & pepper seasoning. Cook until the zucchini is soft.

Transfer to a bowl to cool for about five minutes.

Meanwhile, cook the bacon until it is crisp and set aside.

Add the scallions, eggs and cornmeal to the corn and zucchini and stir to combine.

Add 2 tablespoons of olive oil to the pan over medium heat and drop ½ cup of the mixture into the oil.

Cook as many ½ cup dollops will fit in the pan,

turning once they are browned on the bottom.

Drain the cooked cakes on a layer of paper towels. Continue until all of the batter has been cooked.

Serve these hot with the crumbled goat cheese and cooked bacon.

Bacon Mac and Cheese With Pretzel Topping (Baked in a Cast Iron Skillet)

Ingredients:

¾ pound elbow pasta

1 stick (8 tablespoons) butter

½ cup all-purpose flour

1 teaspoon salt

½ teaspoon freshly cracked black pepper

2 cups whole milk

3 cups cheddar cheese, shredded and divided

1 cup crushed pretzel thins

12 slices of bacon, cooked and crumbled

Directions

Preheat oven to 350.

Cook the pasta in salted water for one minute less than directed on the package. Drain and set aside.

Make roux by melting the butter over medium heat and then whisking in the flour all at once.

Add the seasoning and stir and cook for 3 to 4 minutes.

Slowly whisk in the milk and then constantly stir until the mixture is thickened, about 2 minutes.

If you add the milk too quickly or stop stirring you will get a lumpy, partially cooked roux.

Reduce the heat, add 2 cups of the cheese and simmer until the cheese has melted.

Add the cooked pasta to a 12 inch cast iron skillet over low heat and then stir in the cheese sauce.

Top that with 1 cup of the cheese, the pretzel crumbs and the bacon and then bake for 20 to 25 minutes.

Pan Seared Scallops With Bacon

Ingredients:

3 slices of center cut bacon

1 ½ pound of jumbo sea scallops, about a dozen

¼ teaspoon plus 1/8 teaspoon kosher salt, divided

¼ teaspoon freshly cracked black pepper, divided

1 cup chopped onion

6 cloves of fresh garlic, sliced

One 12 ounce package of fresh baby spinach leaves

4 lemon wedges

Directions:

In a large, cast iron skillet over medium to high heat, cook the bacon until it is crisp.

Remove from pan and set aside to drain.

Reserve one tablespoon of the bacon drippings from the pan.

Pat each scallop with a paper towel and then add to the skillet.

Season with ¼ teaspoon of the salt and 1/8 teaspoon of the pepper and cook over high heat, 2 to 2 ½ minutes per side or until done.

Transfer to a plate tented with foil to keep warm.

Decrease the heat back to medium/high heat once again and add the onion and garlic to the pan.

Cook for three minutes and then add ½ of the spinach. Cook for one minute and then add the other half.

Cook until the spinach is just wilted. Remove from the heat and add the remaining seasoning.

Divide the cooked spinach mixture to four plates and top each serving with 3 of the scallops and ¼ of the bacon.

Serve with the lemon wedges and your choice of side dishes.

Snack Recipes

Baby Potatoes Wrapped in Bacon

Ingredients:

8 slices of bacon cut in half.

16 baby potatoes, your choice of red, yellow or white

Directions:

Preheat oven to 400

Wash each potato and leave the skins on. (You can peel them if you prefer) Wrap each in a slice of the bacon and then bake until the bacon is crispy and the potato is tender, about 40 to 50 minutes.

Bacon and Eggs in Toast Cups

Ingredients:

6 slices of any style of bread

6 slices of any style bacon

6 large eggs

Salt and pepper to taste

Directions:

Preheat oven to 400.

Lightly butter or spray a six cup muffin pan. Trim each slice of the bread, removing all of the crusts and rounding the edges so that it will fit in the pan. Press each slice gently into the prepared muffin pan and bake for about five minutes.

The bread cups should be lightly toasted at this point. Remove from oven and set aside but do not remove from pan.

Put the bacon on a sheet pan that has been lined with parchment paper and bake for 10 minutes or so. You will want the bacon to be mostly cooked but still pliable, not crispy. Remove from oven and allow to cool enough to handle.

Take the slightly cooled bacon and press into the toast cups, gently. Crack one egg into each cup and then decrease the oven temperature to 350.

Bake for 15 to 20 minutes or until the whites of the eggs are set and the yolks are creamy. Remove from pan by running a knife along the edges of each toast cup and then popping them out with a small spoon.

Bacon Wrapped Cocktail Sausages

Ingredients

One 14 ounce package of mini, smoked sausages

One 12 ounce package of bacon

¾ cup of brown sugar (light or dark)

Directions:

Preheat oven to 325.

Line a baking sheet with aluminum foil.

Cut the bacon into thirds. Wrap a piece of the bacon around each of the sausages and then use a toothpick to secure,

Sprinkle each of the bacon wrapped sausages with

the brown sugar and bake for 40 to 45 minutes.

Bacon Cinnamon Rolls

Ingredients

1 can of refrigerated cinnamon roll with icing

8 slices of precooked bacon

Directions:

Preheat the oven to 400.

Spray a 9 inch cake pan with cooking spray and set aside.

Separate the cinnamon rolls and flatten out. Lay one slice of bacon on each of the rolls and then roll back up carefully. Arrange on the prepared pan and bake for 15 to 18 minutes. Remove from oven and frost with the icing.

Thank You For Reading!

OTHER BOOKS BY ELLEN SCOTT

PREVIEW OF ' CANNING AND PRESERVING - All About Canning And Preserving Food In Jars

*** INCLUDES RECIPES!! ***

Introduction

Many people are getting back into home canning and preserving for a number of reasons.

First, it is economical – you can buy produce when it is at its lowest price of the season and then preserve it for the winter months when the prices will dramatically increase.

Second, it is a long standing tradition and one that used to be handed down from generation to generation.

And third, canning and preserving fruits, vegetables and other foods that you are buying from local sources like farmer's markets or growing for yourself are not going to be tainted by chemicals, pesticides and other harmful substances, which means that they are healthier for your family.

A long time ago, there were no supermarkets where exotic fruits and vegetables lined the many shelves.

You ate what you grew in your home garden and that was it. In the winter months, you either ate what you could preserve or you were without fresh greens and the sweet fruits until your garden could be planted again.

Now there are fruits and vegetables trucked or flown in from all over the world, so many foods are available to us year round. With these many foods within easy reach, many people have forgotten all about the tradition of home canning. But, there are some who are returning to the tradition because of the countless benefits that canning and preserving offers them. These include:

Family tradition/quality time

In the past, people would get together and can great batches of surplus fruits and vegetables and spend the entire day, working and laughing together.

Getting together with either your friends and family or your neighbors can be a great new tradition- everyone cans their surplus items and then each member can trade for new recipes they want to try.

The cost savings

Not only are you making sure that nothing goes to waste in your garden when you can or preserve in your home, you are also going to save money during the winter months when the cost of all of these foods are going to be much higher.

The environmental savings

By eating locally produced foods, you are saving the environment plus you are supporting your local economy in the process .

So, everyone benefits!

The less food that has to be shipped to your store means the less trucks that are on the road- less fuel, less wear and tear on the roads and the less air pollution being created.

You also get higher quality, fresher and more nutritious foods in the bargain.

Click Here To Read More!

Or Go To: http://amzn.to/1zCgjH1

25171099R00042

Printed in Great Britain
by Amazon